WITHDRAWN

Earthforms

Deserts

by Kay Jackson

Consultant:
John D. Vitek
Assistant Dean of Graduate Studies
Texas A & M University
College Station, Texas

Mankato, Minnesota

Bridgestone Books are published by Capstone Press,
151 Good Counsel Drive, P.O. Box 669, Mankato, Minnesota 56002.
www.capstonepress.com

Library of Congress Cataloging-in-Publication Data
Jackson, Kay, 1959–
    Deserts / Kay Jackson.
        p. cm.—(Bridgestone books. Earthforms)
    Summary: "Describes deserts, including how they form, desert plants and animals, how people and
weather change deserts, the Sonoran Desert, and the Sahara"—Provided by publisher.
    Includes bibliographical references and index.
    ISBN-13: 978-0-7368-5404-7 (hardcover)
    ISBN-10: 0-7368-5404-5 (hardcover)
    1. Deserts—Juvenile literature. I. Title. II. Bridgestone Books. Earthforms.
GB612.J32 2006
551.41′5—dc22   2005015247

Editorial Credits
Becky Viaene, editor; Juliette Peters, set designer; Patrick D. Dentinger, book designer;
    Anne P. McMullen, illustrator; Jo Miller, photo researcher; Scott Thoms, photo editor

Photo Credits
Bruce Coleman Inc./Steve Solum, 4
Comstock, 1
Houserstock/Dave G. Houser, 12; Ellen Barone, cover
The Image Finders/Werner Lobert, 8
Nature Picture Library/John Cancalosi, 10
Peter Arnold/Frans Lemmens, 18; Matt Meadows, 16; Voltcher/UNEP, 14

1 2 3 4 5 6 11 10 09 08 07 06

Table of Contents

What Are Deserts? 5

How Do Deserts Form? 7

Desert Plants 9

Desert Animals 11

Weather Changes Deserts 13

People Change Deserts 15

The Sonoran Desert 17

The Sahara 19

Deserts on a Map 21

Glossary 22

Read More 23

Internet Sites 23

Index 24

4

What Are Deserts?

Deserts are dry places that get very little rain. Each year, they get less than 10 inches (25 centimeters). Some deserts, like Chile's Atacama Desert, get no rain for years at a time.

Temperatures in most deserts are hot, but a few cold deserts exist. California's hot Mojave Desert may reach 120 degrees Fahrenheit (49 degrees Celsius). China's Gobi Desert can drop to minus 40 degrees Fahrenheit (minus 40 degrees Celsius).

◀ Only small areas of tough plants can live in the hot Mojave Desert.

Desert

How Do Deserts Form?

Most deserts form near the Tropic of Cancer and the Tropic of Capricorn. Warm air rises from the equator, cools, and creates rain. As the cool air moves away from the equator, it drops back toward the surface and is heated. Because rain can't develop in dropping air, deserts form.

Deserts also can form on one side of a mountain. As air rises up a mountain, it cools, and rain falls. As air moves down the mountain, it heats up. Moisture **evaporates** from the air and a desert forms.

◀ Rain falls as clouds rise to cross over the mountains. After crossing, rain clouds disappear as the air drops.

Desert Plants

Desert plants have ways of surviving in the dry **climate**. Creosote bushes and other plants have waxy leaves that store water.

Cactuses do not have leaves. Instead, they store water in their flat stems. Long cactus roots soak up rain. Prickly pear cactus roots can be 15 feet (4.6 meters) long.

On the dry desert, poppy seeds may go months without rain. The seeds need little water to grow. Less than three weeks after rain, yellow and orange poppy flowers bloom.

◀ Just weeks after rain, colorful poppy and lupine flowers bloom next to tall cactuses in the Arizona desert.

Desert Animals

Hot temperatures and lack of water make deserts a tough place to live. Most desert animals are **nocturnal** and avoid daytime heat by staying underground.

Desert animals do not need much water. They get most of their water from food. Squirrels and slow-moving tortoises search for wildflowers and prickly cactuses to eat. Roadrunners dash across the hot land to catch small lizards. Camels can go days without drinking water.

◄ Ground squirrels are careful to avoid cactuses' painful white spines while eating cactus fruit.

Weather Changes Deserts

Although it rarely rains in deserts, water can make big changes. It can turn low, dry spots of land into creeks and small ponds. These creeks and ponds last only a few weeks before they dry up.

Wind can also make big changes to deserts. In some deserts, wind blows sand into large piles called sand dunes. Over time, wind forms new sand dunes and blows others away.

◀ After a storm, rain fills Salt Creek in California's Death Valley. During the hot summer, this creek is usually dry.

People Change Deserts

People change deserts in many ways. Near deserts' edges, people replace **native** plants with crops. These crops can get too dry and cause fires. After the native plants are removed, the land **erodes.** This land adds to the deserts, making them larger.

People also change deserts by adding water. **Canals** carry water from faraway rivers and lakes to dry deserts.

◀ Sand dunes bury crops. Erosion, caused by farming near Africa's Sahara, will make this desert larger.

The Sonoran Desert

The Sonoran Desert lies in northern Mexico and the southwestern United States. This desert gets more rain, and supports more life, than any other desert in North America.

Hundreds of plants and animals live in the Sonoran Desert. Some, including giant saguaro cactuses, live only in this desert. They can grow as tall as a four-story building. Red-tailed hawks sit on top of cactuses. Cactus wrens nest in saguaros' thick skin.

◄ Huge organ pipe and saguaro cactuses cover large areas of the Sonoran Desert in Arizona.

The Sahara

The Sahara is the largest and hottest desert on earth. It covers 3,500,000 square miles (9,065,000 square kilometers). This North African desert is almost as big as the entire United States.

Animals and people live in this desert. Deadly scorpions hide under rocks. Sand foxes hunt lizards. Desert **nomads** lead camels across rocky plains and sand dunes in search of water. The Sahara's people and animals get water from underground springs or wells, called **oases**.

◀ Nomads lead camels across the huge, hot sand dunes of the Sahara.

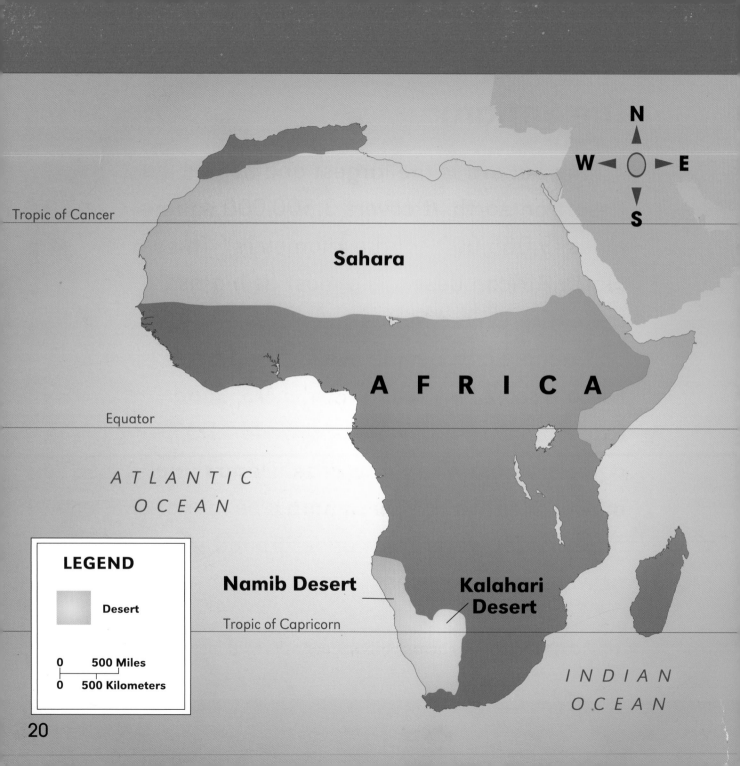

N

W ◀ ⬤ ▶ E

S

Tropic of Cancer

Sahara

A F R I C A

Equator

ATLANTIC
OCEAN

Namib Desert

**Kalahari
Desert**

Tropic of Capricorn

*INDIAN
OCEAN*

LEGEND

Desert

0   500 Miles

0   500 Kilometers

20

Deserts on a Map

Deserts cover one-fifth of the earth's land. Every continent except Europe has deserts. On colored maps, deserts are usually shown in a tan or brown color. Desert names are also labeled on these maps.

On uncolored maps, deserts can be hard to find. Start by looking for the Tropic of Cancer and the Tropic of Capricorn. Many deserts lie close to these lines. Desert names are also labeled on these maps.

◄ Deserts, both big and small, cover much of Africa.

Glossary

canal (kuh-NAL)—a channel that is dug across land, through which water flows

climate (KLYE-mit)—the usual weather in a place

erode (e-RODE)—to wear away; wind and water erode soil and rock.

evaporate (e-VAP-uh-rate)—to change from a liquid to a gas

native (NAY-tiv)—a person, an animal, or a plant that originally lived or grew in a certain place

nocturnal (nok-TUR-nuhl)—active at night

nomad (NOH-mad)—a person who travels from place to place to find food and water

oasis (oh-AY-siss)—a place in a desert where there is water for plants, animals, and people; more than one oasis are called oases.

Read More

Cefrey, Holly. *Deserts.* Reading Power. New York: PowerKids Press, 2003.

Cole, Melissa. *Deserts.* Wild America Habitats. San Diego: Blackbirch Press, 2003.

Internet Sites

FactHound offers a safe, fun way to find Internet sites related to this book. All of the sites on FactHound have been researched by our staff.

Here's how:
1. Visit *www.facthound.com*
2. Type in this special code **0736854045** for age-appropriate sites. Or enter a search word related to this book for a more general search.
3. Click on the **Fetch It** button.

FactHound will fetch the best sites for you!

Index

animals, 11, 17, 19
Atacama Desert, 5

canals, 15
climate, 9
creeks, 13

erosion, 15

formation, 7

Gobi Desert, 5

maps, 21
Mojave Desert, 5
mountains, 7

oases, 19

people, 15, 19
plants, 5, 9, 11, 15, 17
ponds, 13

rain, 5, 7, 9, 13, 17

Sahara, 15, 19
sand dunes, 13, 15, 19
Sonoran Desert, 17

temperatures, 5, 11
tropics, 7, 21

water, 9, 11, 13, 15, 19
wind, 13